Divine Rights and Branding Fights

Divine Rights and Branding Fights

Holy Trademark Wars and Their Earthly Tales

Adam L. Diament

Divine Rights and Branding Fights
Holy Trademark Wars and Their Earthly Tales
Adam L. Diament

Printed by Amazon Direct Publishing
Independently Published

All Rights Reserved. No part of this book may be reproduced or transmitted in any form, by any means, electronic or mechanical, including photocopying, recording or by any information storage and retrieval system, without written permission from the author, except for the inclusion of brief quotations in a review.

Copyright © 2024 Adam L. Diament
First Edition, 2024
Published in the United States of America
ISBN: 9798336127430

About the Author

Adam Diament is a dedicated patent and trademark attorney at the law firm of Nolan Heimann LLP, located in Los Angeles, California. Originally born in Memphis, Tennessee, he relocated with his family to California at the age one, where he has since built his life and career.

Adam earned a B.A. in *Religious Studies* and *Molecular and Cell Biology* from the University of California, Berkeley, in 1997, a Ph.D. in *Genetics* from the University of California, Davis, in 2004, and a law degree from the University of San Diego School of Law in 2008. He lives in Los Angeles, California with his wife Tiffany and daughters Joanna and Audrey.

In his spare time (which he has little of), he enjoys family genealogy research, Lindy Hop swing dancing, playing with his kids, Scrabble, trivia games, and attempting to visit all 482 cities in California. He is also the author of "The Top 10 of Everything Jewish," a book of over 100 top-10 rankings of everything Jewish, "Kosher Patents – 101 Ingenious Inventions to Help Jews be Jewish," and "What Would Jesus Patent? 101 Ingenious Inventions for Christians."

Table of Contents

About the Author iii

Introduction 1

Chapter 1: The Four Horsement of Intellectual Property 3

Chapter 2: Trademark Basics 7

Chapter 3: Not All Marks are Trademarks............................... 11

Chapter 4: Trademark Registration: The Sacred Act of
        Protecting Holy Trademarks................................... 15

Chapter 5: Ascending the Trademark Mount Sinai 21

Chapter 6: Likelihood of Confusion 25

Chapter 7: The Sacred Path to Trademark Defense 29

Chapter 8: Themes in Divine Disputes 41

Chapter 9: Jewish Trademark Disputes................................... 43

Chapter 10: Muslim Trademark Disputes............................... 57

Chapter 11: Christian Trademark Disputes 65

Chapter 12: Scientology Trademark Disputes........................ 93

Chapter 13: Hindu and Buddhist Trademark Disputes 99

Chapter 14: Can't We All Just Coexist? 111

Introduction

Hello, enlightened reader! If you've been drawn to this book, you might expect a solemn journey through the dense jungle of legal jargon that surrounds the world of trademarks. Fear not! While the path may be sprinkled with the occasional serious matter, I promise you an adventure that's as fun as it is enlightening.

Why trademarks, you ask? Because they're the unsung heroes of the business world, often unnoticed yet always present, quietly shaping our choices and loyalties. From the swoosh on your sneakers to the apple on your phone, trademarks are everywhere, whispering their little stories to us.

And, of course, no journey into the land of trademarks would be complete without decoding some of that legal mumbo jumbo—transformed here into plain language, much like turning water into wine.

Given my dual interests in law and religion, this book takes a spirited dive into the divine world of religious and spiritual trademarks. We'll navigate the sanctified waters of trademark law, uncovering how holy symbols and scripture are not just shielded by the heavens but by hefty legal texts too. Watch as we reveal the celestial dance between sacred seals and commercial brands, proving that even the divine has a place in the marketplace.

So lace up your most comfortable intellectual sneakers (logo optional), bring your sense of wonder (and humor), and prepare to embark on a lively journey through the delightful world of trademarks!

Get ready for an enlightening journey that's as filled with chuckles as it is with cherubs, all in the pursuit of demystifying the holy and the trademarked alike.

Disclaimer

This book does not create the sacred covenant of attorney-client relationship. The contents herein do not constitute divine legal counsel and should not be followed as such. Many of the trademarks described are protected, and you may be found in violation of these sacred trademarks if you use the trademarks in certain ways without the owner's blessing. Should you be interested in using any of these marks, please seek guidance from a trademark attorney, as one would seek guidance from a wise and trusted advisor.

* * *

Chapter 1
The Four Horsemen of Intellectual Property

Welcome to the Intellectual Property Carnival, a lively and bustling celebration of creativity and innovation where the wisdom of various religious traditions lights up our journey! Picture four vibrant tents, each showcasing a unique aspect of intellectual property. Join us as we explore the Copyright Cathedral, the Patent Pagoda, the Trade Secret Shrine, and the Trademark Temple. Although this book will focus on the Trademark Temple, you should know the differences between the various kinds of intellectual property.

The Copyright Cathedral: The Creative Guardian Angel

First, we step into the Copyright Cathedral, guarded by the Creative Guardian Angel. Copyrights are the protectors of original works of authorship, much like the divine protection granted by guardian angels. They grant creators exclusive rights to use and distribute their works, ensuring they can control how their creations are shared and monetized.

Copyrights safeguard sacred texts and ensure they remain unaltered and respected. From J.K. Rowling's "Harry Potter" books to Taylor Swift's latest album, copyrights ensure that creators are rewarded for their creativity and that their works are not copied or distributed without permission.

The Patent Pagoda: The Innovation Deity

Moving along, we find ourselves at the Patent Pagoda, watched over by the Innovation Deity. Patents are the protectors of inventions and innovations, granting inventors the exclusive right to make, use, and sell their creations for a certain period, usually 20 years.

Patents encourage innovation by rewarding inventors with temporary exclusivity to their creations, much like the blessings bestowed by gods in various mythologies to their devotees. From the light bulb to the smartphone, patents have protected some of the most significant inventions in history. They come in three types: utility patents (for new processes or devices), design patents (for new original designs), and plant patents (for new plant varieties). Whether you've invented a groundbreaking gadget, a unique furniture design, or a new type of rose, patents provide divine protection.

The Trade Secret Shrine: The Silent Sentinel

Next, we reach the Trade Secret Shrine, overseen by the Silent Sentinel. Trade secrets protect confidential business information that provides a competitive edge. Like the hidden knowledge in esoteric traditions, trade secrets are not registered with any government agency but depend on their secrecy for protection.

Famous examples of trade secrets include the recipe for Coca-Cola and the formula for WD-40. These valuable pieces of information are closely guarded, much like the mystical secrets in ancient temples. If the secret gets out, the protection is lost, so confidentiality is paramount.

The Trademark Temple: The Branding Buddha

And last, the focus of this book, we enter the Trademark Temple, where the Branding Buddha presides. Trademarks are the divine protectors of identity, safeguarding symbols, names, logos, and slogans that distinguish goods or services from one another. They are like the sacred symbols of religious sects, which signify specific meanings and invoke particular associations.

Trademarks ensure that when you see a particular logo or hear a specific jingle, you instantly recognize the product or service. They prevent brand confusion and maintain the integrity of a company's identity. Without trademarks, we might mistake Pepsi for Coke, or think every pair of jeans is made by Levi's. Imagine the chaos! Like the distinct symbols of different faiths, trademarks keep the marketplace orderly and recognizable.

The Grand Finale: Comparing the Divine Champions

Now that we've visited all the tents, let's compare our intellectual property champions in a fun, carnival-style showdown:

- **Copyrights**: Guard creative works like books, music, and films, rewarding creators for their originality and effort.
- **Patents**: Shield inventions and innovations, encouraging inventors to bring new ideas to life by granting exclusive rights.

- **Trade Secrets**: Protect confidential business information, relying on secrecy to provide a competitive edge.
- **Trademarks**: Protect brand identity with logos, names, and slogans, ensuring consumers know exactly what they're getting.

Each type of intellectual property plays a crucial role in the vibrant ecosystem of creativity and commerce. They ensure that inventors, creators, and businesses can thrive and continue to innovate, entertain, and provide value to society. As we leave the Intellectual Property Carnival, remember that while these champions have different roles and strengths, they all work together to protect the fruits of human ingenuity. So, whether you're an inventor, an artist, a business owner, or just a curious soul, the world of intellectual property has something fascinating to offer.

Chapter 2
Trademark Basics

What in Heaven's Name is a Trademark?

Imagine you're strolling through a bustling marketplace and your gaze falls upon a sign adorned with a luminous golden arch. Instantly, thoughts of tasty burgers and fries fill your mind. That, dear pilgrim, is the power of a trademark. It acts like a beacon of light, guiding your thoughts and choices with just a symbol, word, or melody. It's a sacred mark, legally anointed, that signals the divine presence of a particular creator behind a product.

The Divine Elements of a Trademark

A trademark can manifest in many miraculous forms—a holy phrase, a unique aroma (indeed, even fragrances can be blessed as trademarks!), a logo, or a celestial combination of colors. These elements are not chosen by mere chance; they are divine symbols crafted to evoke recognition and devotion. Consider them the sacred relics in the temple of commerce, each adding a unique essence to the brand's divine aura.

The Heavenly Mission of a Trademark

Why do these sacred symbols exist? They serve to vanquish the demons of confusion and deception. Trademarks help the faithful discern the true origin of a product, ensuring that you don't mistakenly acquire a forgery. They stand as valiant protectors in the realm of commerce, keeping watch over the integrity of brand identity.

Registering a Trademark: The Divine Decree

Securing a trademark is not as simple as proclaiming, "It is mine!" Rather, one must seek the divine decree by registering it with the earthly authorities—akin to seeking a blessing from the high priests in ancient times. This process involves demonstrating that your trademark is unique and not merely an imitation of another's divine sign. Once sanctioned, you are endowed with the exclusive right to wield your sacred emblem in the marketplaces of the world (or at least in the country of registration).

Trademark Crusades: Defending the Faith

Even in the harmonious lands of commerce, conflicts arise when someone unlawfully wields a trademark. These are the times for righteous battles in the courts of law. Fear not, for if your trademark is just and pure, the scales of justice will tip in your favor, restoring peace and order in the commercial realms.

The Immortality of a Trademark

Unlike mortal beings, trademarks can achieve immortality, enduring as long as they are revered and upheld in the marketplace. So long as the masses continue to cherish your blessed products and employ your sanctified apps, your trademark can ascend to eternal life, forever revered.

The Eternal Pilgrimage Continues

By now, you should recognize that a trademark is more than a mere label; it is a beacon of quality, a pillar of faith, and a protector of the sacred. As we continue our spiritual journey through the mystical landscape of trademark law, keep your heart open and your spirit attuned—there's divine magic in the air!

So, remain steadfast, and remember, behind every humble trademark lies a grand saga of legal valor, ceaselessly working to deliver the products you adore with a touch of divine grace. Let's turn the page and continue our blessed exploration together!

Chapter 3
Not All Marks Are Trademarks

Welcome back, faithful travelers! As we continue our sacred journey through the realm of trademarks, let us pause and ponder a celestial question: Are all marks "trademarks"? Gather around the campfire of knowledge, as we explore the mystical landscape where divine symbols and commercial marks mingle — and learn why not all that glitters in the marketplace is trademarked!

The Divine Essence of Marks

In the beginning, there were marks. These were not mere signs, but symbols imbued with spiritual power and deep meaning. From the ancient carvings on temple walls to the intricate designs on sacred scrolls, marks have always been with us, guiding, protecting, and enlightening. But beware, dear pilgrims — not all marks serve the gods of commerce!

Sacred Symbols: The Cross, The Crescent, and The Star of David

Consider the holy symbols that light our spiritual paths: the Cross, the Crescent, and the Star of David. Each of these celestial icons holds a profound connection to the faithful, representing deep religious truths and guiding millions in their spiritual lives.

- **The Cross**: A symbol of sacrifice and salvation, seen atop churches and worn as a solemn reminder of spiritual grace.
- **The Crescent**: Gracing the flags and emblems of nations, it reflects the cycles of the moon and marks holy Islamic festivals.
- **The Star of David**: A symbol of Jewish identity and endurance, this six-pointed star embodies a rich tapestry of history and faith.

These sacred symbols transcend mere commercial value, serving as beacons of faith rather than badges of trade.

When Marks Become Trademarks

Now, let us explore when a mark crosses the sacred boundary and becomes a trademark. A trademark, blessed by the laws of commerce, is a mark used to identify and distinguish goods or services in the marketplace. It's a sign that a merchant or a maker uses to tell the world, "This is mine, and it is good."

Imagine a bakery named "Heavenly Delights" that uses a stylized angel as its logo, or a clothing line called "Crescent Threads" with a unique crescent moon tag on each garment. Here, the celestial symbols have taken on a commercial mantle, serving both the gods of commerce and the muse of marketing.

The Divine Line: Not All Marks Are Trademarks

It's crucial, our wise travelers, to discern the line between the divine and the commercial. While a cross, a crescent, or a Star of David can be part of a trademark, their deeper, sacred meanings are not for sale. They guide the spirit, not the transaction. When used in trademarks, they tread the fine line between reverence and commerce, always reminding us of their higher calling. Sometimes there are grey areas. Is the word "Mormon" a trademark of a specific religious entity that you are not allowed to use without permission? Or is it a word like "Protestant" or "Jewish," where it only describes a belief system that no one has the rights to? We'll get more into that later!

The Holy Conclusion

As we wrap up this chapter under the starlit sky of understanding, remember, not all marks are trademarks. Some are divine symbols, etched in the soul of humanity, while others serve in the bustling marketplaces of the world.

Stay tuned, dear pilgrims, for our journey is far from over. Let us continue to tread lightly on this sacred ground, always mindful of the divine distinction between marks that guide our faith and trademarks that guide our choices in the marketplace. Onward we go, with enlightenment on our minds!

Chapter 4
Trademark Registration: The Sacred Act of Protecting Holy Trademarks

Rejoice, pilgrims of the marketplace! As we journey further into the mystical realm of trademarks, let us delve into the sacred rite known as trademark registration. Why, you may ask, would a religious group need to partake in such earthly rituals? Gather round as we explore the heavenly benefits and potential perils of not securing these celestial seals in the world of commerce.

The Holy Process of Trademark Registration

Trademark registration is akin to a knighthood ceremony for your brand's symbols and phrases. It is the process where the worldly powers that be (also known as the United States Patent and Trademark Office) grants your mark the divine right to rule over its commercial kingdom exclusively. By registering, you declare to the world that this particular symbol or phrase is yours alone to use in spreading your sacred message or selling your blessed goods.

Why Even the Divine Need to Register

Imagine a world where two congregations, unbeknownst to each other, choose the same symbol to represent their spiritual missions—let's say, a radiant dove holding an olive branch. Without registration, both could unintentionally sow confusion among the faithful, diluting the divine message and perhaps even leading to unholy disputes. By registering, a religious group can ensure that their emblem of peace is uniquely associated with their teachings, thus preserving the purity and power of their spiritual brand.

The Heavenly Advantages of Registration

- **Divine Protection**: Just as ancient warriors marked their shields with holy symbols for protection, registering a trademark shields your brand against misuse and misrepresentation. It protects the faithful from being misled by false prophets or counterfeit goods masquerading under your sacred name.

- **Commercial Blessings**: Registered trademarks can be a source of funding for religious groups. Through licensing agreements, others can use your registered

mark in a manner that supports your mission, all while contributing financially to your holy endeavors.
- **Entire Country Pilgrimage**: With a registered trademark, your symbol or phrase can travel safely across state borders without having to re-register in every state.

The Perils of Neglecting Registration

Failing to register a trademark is like leaving the doors of your temple unlocked, inviting all manner of chaos and confusion. Unregistered marks are vulnerable to misuse and exploitation. Without the legal sanctity of registration, defending a trademark in court can be a more costly crusade, potentially diverting precious resources away from your spiritual missions.

A Cautionary Tale

Imagine a humble, yet vibrant religious community known as the Serenity Sect. Founded on principles of peace, tranquility, and harmony with nature, this sect developed a unique symbol—a serene tree under a starlit sky, which resonated deeply with people across the world. As the sect's popularity grew, so did the visibility of their emblem.

One day, a large international corporation, EcoWear, searching for a new logo for their line of outdoor clothing, stumbled upon the Serenity Sect's symbol. Seeing that it was not registered as a trademark and misled by its widespread but unofficial use, EcoWear adapted it for their latest range of products.

The Fallout

- **Confusion Among the Faithful**: The Serenity Sect's members were bewildered to see their sacred symbol on advertisements for hiking apparel and camping

gear. The symbol's religious significance was diluted, and the line between spirituality and commerce blurred disastrously.
- **Commercial Exploitation**: Without the legal protections afforded by a registered trademark, EcoWear capitalized massively on the symbol, placing it on everything from t-shirts to tents. The market was soon saturated with the emblem, now stripped of its original sanctity.
- **Loss of Identity**: The sect struggled to maintain its identity as the symbol, once a beacon of their beliefs, became more associated with outdoor sports and leisure rather than spiritual serenity.

Realizing the gravity of the situation, the Serenity Sect attempted to reclaim their symbol through legal means. However, their lack of a registered trademark severely hampered their efforts.

- **Legal Complexities**: The sect found themselves entangled in complex legal battles, facing the challenge of proving that the symbol was synonymous solely with their religious practices and not a generic image that could be used by anyone.
- **Financial Burden**: The legal fees quickly mounted, draining resources that could have been used for community projects and outreach programs. The financial strain added to the sect's woes, diverting their focus from spiritual development to courtroom battles.
- **Public Perception**: The prolonged legal disputes and the association of their sacred symbol with commercial products caused public confusion and eroded the credibility of the Serenity Sect. The damage to their spiritual image was profound and possibly irreparable.

While our tale is fictional, the risks it illustrates are very real. For the Serenity Sect and similar groups, the road back to reclaiming their symbol's sanctity is long and fraught with challenges. But with the right legal protections in place, future calamities of this nature can be averted, allowing religious groups to focus on nurturing their spiritual missions without earthly encumbrances.

Thus, let this story serve as a stark reminder: in the realm of trademarks, an ounce of prevention is truly worth a pound of cure. May all spiritual symbols remain hallowed, respected, and legally protected.

Concluding Benediction

As we close this chapter, let us remember that in the bustling marketplaces of our world, even the divine must sometimes engage in the earthly practice of registration to protect and prosper. May your trademarks be as your faith—strong, recognized, and respected across lands and generations.

Stay vigilant, dear pilgrims, for the path to trademark enlightenment is both sacred and strategic. Let us proceed with wisdom and joy, ensuring our marks are not just made, but divinely sanctioned and secured!

Chapter 5
Ascending the Trademark Mount Sinai

Not all trademarks are created equal! Some are strong marks, where you can stop someone from using your mark, even if the mark isn't exactly the same as yours. Other marks may be weak, where you get no protection at all. Mark strength has been groups into five categories, in order of no strength to Samson strong!

1. **Generic - The Common Folk**

    At the base of our mountain sit the generics. These are the everyday manna of the trademark world, common words like "Bread" for a loaf or "Computer" for, well, computers. These terms are free for all to use, as they lack any special branding blessing. If you try to register these marks, the Trademark Office will reject the application.

2. **Descriptive - The Informative Disciples**

    Climbing a step, we meet the descriptives. These terms reveal something specific about the product. "Sharp" for TVs with clear images or "QuickPrint" for a swift printing service. Descriptives can ascend to trademark protection, but only if they acquire a secondary meaning among the faithful — that is, if people start associating "QuickPrint" not just with any quick printing service, but specifically with your printing ministry!

3. **Suggestive - The Clever Apostles**

    Further up, we find suggestive marks, which stir the imagination without revealing all. They hint at a quality without describing it outright. Consider "Jaguar" for fast cars or "Coppertone" for sunscreens. These marks are inherently distinctive enough to receive trademark protection because they require a leap of thought to connect the mark with the product.

4. **Arbitrary - The Quirky Saints**

    Near the summit, reside the arbitrary marks. These are common words that bear no logical relationship to the products they represent. "Apple" for computers? A delightfully arbitrary choice! These marks are strong because they are memorable and unexpected, making them excellent candidates for full trademark sanctification.

5. **Fanciful - The Archangels of Creativity**

   At the pinnacle of our climb sit the fanciful marks. These are the kings and queens of the trademark realm, born from pure imagination. Think "Xerox" for copiers and "Kodak" for cameras. Fanciful marks are the strongest type of trademark because they are invented words with no meaning other than as a brand identity.

The Parable of Our Ascent

As we descend back to the earthly realm from our climb, let us reflect on the parable of our trademark journey: the strength of a mark lies not just in the word, but in its distinctiveness and the sacred space it occupies among consumers. Whether you're a humble generic or a regal fanciful, each mark has its ordained place in the marketplace. The divine challenge is to ascend as high as possible on the ladder of trademark strength, securing a unique spot in the hearts and minds of your flock.

So, next time you coin a brand name, ponder where it rests on this sacred ladder. Is it supporting the base, or is it reaching towards the heavens? Regardless of its position, make it memorable, make it yours, and watch it rise!

Chapter 6
Likelihood of Confusion

In the grand theater of trademarks, "likelihood of confusion" is the leading character. It determines whether you are even allowed to register your mark. It also determines whether someone else is infringing your mark. This star-studded term asks a simple question: might a reasonably attentive consumer mistake one brand's goods or services for those of another because of the mark? It's like mistaking a sugar cookie for a snickerdoodle—they look alike at a glance, but the taste tells the truth!

Factors of Likelihood of Confusion

Like a grand procession in a cathedral, the analysis of likelihood of confusion parades several doctrinal factors before us. Let us illuminate a few key revelations:

1. **Similarity of the Marks – Twins or Distant Cousins?**

    Are the marks identical twins, or do they just share a family resemblance? We examine their appearance, sound, and meaning. Even a slight change in recipe can make a big difference. For instance, "Kit Kat" vs. "Kik Kat" – close enough to make you look twice if they're both in the candy aisle! The more similar the mark, the more likely you won't get your similar mark registered.

2. **Similarity of the Products or Services – Same Party, Different Corners**

    Do the marks compete in the same industry playground? Sneakers vs. sandals? Or Sneakers vs. computers? The closer they are in product line or service, the higher the chance of a mix-up. Marks can be identical if the goods are not related at all. Think "Dove" for chocolate bars and "Dove" for soap, which can both co-exist as registered marks because they're for very different goods.

3. **Strength of the Mark – The Signature Outfit**

    How distinctive is the trademark? Is it a generic white tee or a dazzling bespoke suit? The stronger or more distinctive the mark—think Nike's swoosh or McDonald's golden arches—the more likely it is to be recognized, the more protection it garners.

4. **Likelihood of Expansion – Future Fashion Lines**

    Will one brand expand into the other's turf? If there's a chance that one might dip their toes into new product pools, the waters of confusion could get muddy. A shoe company may venture into the sock business, but probably wouldn't venture into the air conditioner business.

5. **Evidence of Actual Confusion – When Consumers Can't Tell the Difference**

    Have there been documented mix-ups among the congregation? Actual confusion is like witnessing a mistaken prayer—it's direct evidence that the similarity is leading the faithful astray. Do you have evidence that people are attending a different church, thinking that it's your church?

6. **Consumer Sophistication – The Savvy Shopper**

    Are the customers discerning connoisseurs or casual shoppers? The level of consumer care matters. Buying a car involves more thought than snagging a candy bar at the checkout. The more the consumers are sophisticated, the lower the chance there would be confusion.

Plot Twist: The Balancing Act of Belief

Like any profound parable, the analysis of likelihood of confusion is not a straight path but a balancing act, weighing all factors to discern if, overall, there's a chance the faithful might reach for one sacred symbol thinking it's another. It's not merely about checking doctrinal boxes but feeling out the overall spirit of the marketplace. The first two factors above are the most important (similarity of mark, and similarity of goods/services), but in close calls, numerous other factors, (even more than the six above) can make or break your case.

The Moral of Our Story

Navigating trademark infringement is a blend of divine intuition and earthly evidence. It teaches brands to tread the hallowed grounds carefully, ensuring their trademarks are not only unique but also reverently clear of encroaching upon their neighbors' consecrated grounds.

So next time you envision a radiant brand mark, remember the lessons from the likelihood of confusion liturgy: make it distinctive, make it yours, and always keep a vigilant eye on the market's mosaic.

Chapter 7
The Sacred Path to Trademark Defense

Here, we'll explore the sacred paths of trademark defenses, where even the mightiest of brand guardians can find solace and strategy amidst claims of infringement. Armed with wit and wisdom, let us embark on a whimsical journey through the ethereal realms of legal defenses, complete with parables and hypotheticals!

Nominative Fair-Use
Hypothetical Example: "Shrine of Harmony"

Background: In the heart of a bustling city stood two grand places of worship: the Temple of Serenity and the Shrine of Harmony. Both religious groups had their distinct practices and symbols, yet they coexisted peacefully for decades. The Temple of Serenity, known for its symbol of a serene lotus, had followers who embraced meditation and mindfulness. The Shrine of Harmony, symbolized by a radiant sun, attracted devotees seeking balance and inner peace through various rituals and chants.

Trademark Dispute: One sunny afternoon, the Temple of Serenity discovered that the Shrine of Harmony had used their sacred lotus symbol on pamphlets advertising a joint meditation event. The Temple leaders were furious, believing that their symbol had been misappropriated. They felt that the Shrine's use of the lotus could confuse followers and diminish the unique identity of their own practices. Consequently, they decided to take legal action and sued the Shrine of Harmony for trademark infringement.

Defense: The Shrine of Harmony, represented by their wise legal advisor, Brother Amos, decided to invoke the defense of nominative fair use. Brother Amos argued that the use of the lotus symbol was necessary to describe the event accurately and to inform the public that the Temple of Serenity was participating in the joint meditation.

Legal Arguments: In the courtroom, the air was thick with anticipation as both sides presented their cases. The Temple of Serenity's lawyer passionately explained how the lotus symbol was integral to their identity and how its misuse by the Shrine could lead to confusion among their followers.

Brother Amos, calm and collected, then took the floor. He began by acknowledging the importance of the lotus symbol to the Temple of Serenity. He argued that the Shrine of Harmony had no intention of misleading anyone or diluting the Temple's brand. Instead, their use of the lotus symbol was purely nominative – it was necessary to refer to the Temple of Serenity in the context of the joint event.

Brother Amos laid out the three criteria for nominative fair use:

1. **The product or service in question must be one not readily identifiable without use of the trademark.** He explained that describing the event without mentioning the Temple of Serenity and its lotus symbol would have been impossible and confusing for the community.
2. **Only so much of the mark or marks may be used as is reasonably necessary to identify the product or service.** The Shrine had used the lotus symbol sparingly, just enough to indicate the Temple's participation in the event.
3. **The user must do nothing that would suggest sponsorship or endorsement by the trademark holder.** The pamphlets clearly indicated that the event was a collaboration, with no suggestion that the Temple of Serenity endorsed the Shrine's practices or vice versa.

Outcome: The judge, after carefully considering the arguments, sided with the Shrine of Harmony. She ruled that the use of the lotus symbol was indeed nominative fair use. The symbol was used in good faith to describe the Temple's involvement in the joint event, without implying any endorsement or causing confusion about the origin of the services.

Descriptive Fair-Use
Hypothetical Example: "Sacred Leaf"

Background: Nestled in the picturesque valley of Everfaith, two vibrant religious groups thrived side by side: the Order of the Sacred Leaf and the Fellowship of the Blessed Brook. The Order of the Sacred Leaf, known for their green leaf emblem, emphasized the connection between nature and spirituality. The Fellowship of the Blessed Brook, represented by a blue brook symbol, focused on the purity and flow of life's spiritual journey.

For years, these two groups coexisted harmoniously, often sharing stories and celebrations. However, a minor misunderstanding soon blossomed into a full-blown legal drama, showcasing the nuances of trademark law within a religious setting.

Trademark Dispute: One spring morning, the Order of the Sacred Leaf discovered that the Fellowship of the Blessed Brook had used the term "sacred leaf" in a series of their new pamphlets. These pamphlets were meant to describe the importance of natural elements in their rituals. The Order felt that their cherished term was being encroached upon and that this usage could lead to confusion about the source of the spiritual guidance offered by each group.

Alarmed by this perceived infringement, the Order of the Sacred Leaf decided to sue the Fellowship of the Blessed Brook for trademark infringement, claiming that the use of "sacred leaf" in the pamphlets was a direct violation of their trademark.

Defense: The Fellowship of the Blessed Brook, under the astute guidance of their ever-optimistic legal advisor, Sister Clara, decided to use the defense of descriptive fair use. Sister Clara argued that the term "sacred leaf" was used purely in a descriptive manner to explain their rituals and not to mislead or confuse anyone.

Legal Arguments: As the case unfolded in the hallowed halls of the Everfaith Courthouse, both sides presented their arguments with fervor. The Order of the Sacred Leaf's attorney highlighted the significance of their trademarked term, emphasizing how it was central to their identity and spiritual message.

Sister Clara, representing the Fellowship, stepped forward with her trademark smile. She began by respecting the Order's deep connection to the term "sacred leaf" but pointed out that the term was also a common descriptive phrase used to talk about holy leaves in various spiritual contexts.

She laid out the key points of descriptive fair use:

1. **The term is used in its primary, descriptive sense.** Sister Clara explained that the Fellowship's pamphlets used "sacred leaf" to describe the ritualistic use of leaves in their ceremonies, a common practice in many spiritual traditions.
2. **The term is used in good faith and not as a trademark.** The Fellowship had no intention of adopting the term "sacred leaf" as a brand identifier but merely used it to describe an element of their spiritual practices.
3. **There is no attempt to create confusion or suggest endorsement.** The pamphlets clearly outlined the Fellowship's practices without implying any connection to or endorsement by the Order of the Sacred Leaf.

Outcome: After listening to both sides, the judge took a moment to reflect on the arguments presented. The atmosphere in the courtroom was electric with anticipation. Finally, the judge ruled in favor of the Fellowship of the Blessed Brook, agreeing that their use of "sacred leaf" was indeed descriptive fair use.

The ruling was met with relief and understanding. The Order of the Sacred Leaf, though initially disheartened, recognized the fairness of the decision and acknowledged the descriptive nature of the term as used by the Fellowship.

Parody
Hypothetical Example: "Saint Bucks Coffee"

Background: "Saint Bucks Coffee" is a quirky new coffee shop located near a bustling university campus, known for its tongue-in-cheek approach to religion and coffee culture. The shop's logo features a stylized saint holding a coffee cup, with a design that mimics the famous "Starbucks" logo, including a similar green color scheme and circular design. However, instead of a mermaid, the "Saint Bucks" logo depicts a cheerful, cartoonish saint with coffee beans for a halo.

Trademark Dispute: Starbucks notices the "Saint Bucks Coffee" logo and files a lawsuit against the coffee shop, claiming trademark infringement. They argue that the parody is too close to its own well-known mark, potentially leading to confusion among customers about the relationship between the two brands.

Defense: "Saint Bucks Coffee" argues that their logo is a clear parody of the Starbucks logo, designed to critique both the commercialization of religious imagery and the omnipresence of major coffee chains. They claim the logo uses humor to highlight the contrast between the sacred and the everyday mundanity of grabbing a coffee, thus fulfilling the parody's purpose of critique and humor.

Legal Arguments: The defense presents the following arguments:

1. **Distinct Visual Presentation**: While the structure of the logo mirrors Starbucks, the inclusion of a cartoonish saint and coffee bean halo uses overtly humorous and exaggerated elements that clearly differentiate it from the more sophisticated and worldly Starbucks image.
2. **Lack of Consumer Confusion**: "Saint Bucks Coffee" provides evidence from customer surveys showing that their patrons recognize the logo as a humorous

take and do not believe the shop is affiliated with or endorsed by Starbucks.
3. **Commentary Purpose**: The defense emphasizes that the parody logo comments on the cultural and commercial blending of religious iconography with consumer culture, thereby falling under the protections afforded to parodic works that use humor to provide social commentary.

Outcome: Depending on how convincingly "Saint Bucks Coffee" can demonstrate that their use of the parody logo clearly serves as both a joke and a critique, and that it does not confuse consumers about brand affiliation, the court may rule in their favor. The successful application of the parody defense hinges on proving that the parody is evident, intentional, and understood by the consuming public. Parody used to be a stronger defense until the case of Jack Daniel's v. VIP Products (Bad Spaniels), where the Supreme Court weakened the parody defense.

Lack of Likelihood of Confusion
Hypothetical Example: "Trinity Trekking Boots"

Background: Jacob, an avid hiker and entrepreneur, decides to launch a line of durable hiking boots designed for serious adventurers. He names his product "Trinity Trekking Boots," inspired by the challenging three-peak trails popular among seasoned hikers. The logo for Trinity Trekking Boots features a stylized mountain with three peaks.

Trademark Dispute: "Trinity Treads," a well-established manufacturer of religious-themed footwear, holds a trademark on the name "Trinity" for their line of church-appropriate shoes. They file a lawsuit against Jacob, claiming that his "Trinity Trekking Boots" infringes on their trademark, potentially confusing consumers.

Defense: Jacob argues that there is no likelihood of confusion between "Trinity Trekking Boots" and "Trinity Treads." His defense is rooted in the distinct differences in the target market, product use, and branding imagery.

Legal Arguments: Jacob's defense includes several cheerful and clear points:

1. **Distinct Target Markets**: Jacob demonstrates that "Trinity Trekking Boots" are marketed towards outdoor enthusiasts looking for rugged, durable footwear specifically for hiking, whereas "Trinity Treads" targets a more sedate demographic interested in stylish, comfortable footwear suitable for church and community gatherings.
2. **Different Product Use**: He emphasizes that the intended use of the boots (outdoor, rough terrain) is vastly different from that of "Trinity Treads" (indoor, polished floors), making it unlikely that consumers would confuse the two when making a purchase.
3. **Visual and Thematic Differences**: The logo and packaging of "Trinity Trekking Boots" feature mountainous and adventurous themes, contrasting

sharply with the peaceful, serene imagery used by "Trinity Treads," which often includes doves and church windows.

Outcome: Depending on Jacob's ability to convincingly present these distinctions, the court might find that the differences in target audience, product use, and branding elements sufficiently reduce the risk of consumer confusion, siding with Jacob and allowing him to continue his adventurous branding.

Prior Use Defense
Hypothetical Example – "HolyRoller Skates"

Background: Benny, an enthusiastic roller skate designer and devout member of his community, owns a small but beloved roller skate shop known for its quirky, religious-themed roller skates. Benny's signature product, "HolyRoller Skates," features wheels designed like stained glass windows and colorful patterns inspired by church art. Benny has been selling these skates from his shop in a small town since 2010, relying solely on local fame and word-of-mouth.

Trademark Dispute: "Divine Glide," a large national sporting goods company, launches a line of roller skates under the same name "HolyRoller" in 2022. They soon discover Benny's shop and send him a cease and desist letter, claiming he is infringing on their newly registered trademark.

Defense: Benny responds with a prior use defense, arguing that he has been using the "HolyRoller Skates" mark commercially in his local area long before "Divine Glide" registered the trademark and began using it nationally.

Legal Arguments: Benny's defense is both spirited and straightforward:

1. **Documented Early Use**: Benny provides sales receipts, advertisements in local church bulletins, and photographs of his shop featuring the "HolyRoller Skates" branding that date back to 2010.
2. **Good Faith Use**: Benny emphasizes that his use of the name was in good faith, inspired by his passion for both roller skating and his faith, long before "Divine Glide" entered the market.

Outcome: If Benny can convincingly show that his prior use of the "HolyRoller Skates" trademark was significant, continuous, and in good faith within his locale, the court may recognize his right to continue using the mark in his area. "Divine Glide" would then be prevented from shutting down

Benny's use of the mark where he has established recognition and goodwill.

Chapter 8
Themes in Divine Disputes

Misuse of Sacred Symbols

Often at the heart of disputes is the use—or misuse—of symbols that hold profound spiritual significance. The central question: Can a symbol that carries deep religious meaning be restricted to a single entity's use?

Commercialization Concerns

As religious symbols find their way onto merchandise and in advertisements, many organizations grapple with the commercialization of what they hold sacred. These cases question the limits of turning faith into a brand.

Inter-Denominational Conflicts

Sometimes the conflict is within the house of faith itself, between different groups claiming rights over the same religious heritage. These disputes can be particularly complex, weaving through doctrinal differences to understand who, if anyone, holds the trademark rights.

Lighter Side of Legal Battles

Despite the serious undertones, there's a lighter side to these divine disputes. They bring together a colorful cast of legal minds, theologians, historians, and even marketing gurus, each interpreting ancient texts and modern laws. Picture a courtroom where cross-examinations involve discussions on theology and brand identity—certainly not your everyday legal drama!

Chapter 9
Jewish Trademark Disputes

Judaism is one of the world's oldest religions, centered around the belief in a single, all-powerful God who created the universe. Originating with the ancient Hebrews, Judaism's teachings are rooted in the Torah, the first five books of the Hebrew Bible, which contains the laws and commandments that guide Jewish life. Jewish traditions include the observance of the Sabbath, a day of rest and worship, as well as various holidays like Passover, which commemorates the Israelites' exodus from Egypt, and Hanukkah, celebrating the rededication of the Second Temple in Jerusalem.

Beyond religious practices, Judaism is also rich in cultural and ethical values, emphasizing justice, kindness, and the importance of community. Jewish people often gather in synagogues for prayer and study, and many Jewish homes feature rituals like lighting the Shabbat candles or saying blessings over wine and bread. With a history that spans thousands of years, Judaism continues to be a vibrant and evolving tradition, fostering a sense of identity, continuity, and connection among Jewish people around the world.

Judaism is known for its special dietary rules called "kashrut." These rules make sure the food is "kosher," meaning it's fit and fabulous for those who follow them. The laws of kashrut include what species are forbidden, the proper slaughtering of animals, and not mixing milk and meat products together (bye-bye cheeseburgers!). Sounds simple enough, right? But, oh no! Sometimes, there's drama in this delicious kingdom—like when someone uses a trademarked kosher certification symbol without permission. It's like a food fight, but with lawyers!

Union of Orthodox Jewish Congregations of America
v.
The Wilder Spice Company

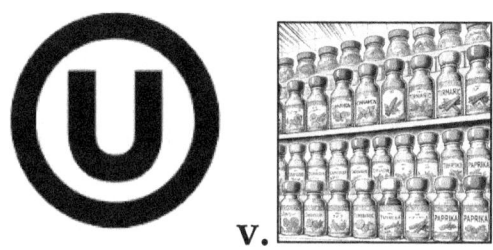

v.

Background

The Orthodox Union (OU), a prestigious and well-respected kosher certification agency, found themselves in a pickle. They discovered that The Wilder Spice Company was using their famous OU mark on their products without permission. This OU mark is like the superhero cape of kosher certification—everyone recognizes it and trusts it to mean that the food has met all the strict kosher requirements.

Legal Dispute

The OU wasn't about to let this slide. They filed a lawsuit, and here's where the drama unfolds. The OU argued that Wilder Spice's unauthorized use of their mark could confuse consumers. Imagine thinking you're buying a kosher-approved spice, only to find out it's an imposter! The OU also claimed that Wilder Spice knew exactly what they were doing. Even after being told to stop, they continued using the mark. That's like being told to stop throwing a party in your neighbor's yard and just cranking up the music instead!

Wilder Spice at first said that they were using ingredients in their own spice mixes that already had the OU stamp approval, and they mistakenly thought it was ok to put the

OU stamp on their own spicy mix products. Adding more spice to the story, Wilder Spice allegedly used a forged letter of certification to support their kosher claims. That's like trying to sneak into a concert with a fake ticket!

Outcome

The United States District Court for the District of Maryland stepped in to sort out this kosher chaos. The court sided with the OU, laying down the law with these key points:

- **Willful Infringement:** The court found that Wilder Spice's infringement was indeed willful. They knew they were out of bounds but kept playing the game.
- **Statutory Damages:** Because of their willful missteps, Wilder Spice had to pay up—big time. The court awarded the OU a whopping $300,000 in damages. That's a lot of spices!
- **Additional Costs:** On top of the damages, Wilder Spice also had to cover attorney's fees and other legal costs, which added up to about $19,198.53. Talk about adding salt to the wound!

This case serves as a spicy reminder that kosher certification marks are serious business. Misuse them, and you might end up in a legal stew, facing hefty fines and a tarnished reputation. So, if you're thinking of sneaking a kosher mark onto your product without permission, remember the tale of Wilder Spice and think twice!

Organized Kashruth Laboratories (OK Labs)
v.
Kosher Overseers of America (KOA)

v.

Factual Background

The trademark tangle between KOA (Kosher Overseers Association of America, Inc.) and OK Labs is quite the kosher conundrum! Both parties are vying to mark their territory in the world of kosher certification, but their logos might be a bit too similar for comfort.

Legal Dispute

OK Labs, which has been proudly stamping its kosher goods with a "Circle-K" mark for years, wasn't too pleased when KOA came along with an "encircled half-moon K" mark that they wanted registered. Understandably, OK Labs felt this new mark could cause some serious consumer confusion—like mistaking a bagel for a bialy!

Outcome

The Trademark Trial and Appeal Board (TTAB) took a good, hard look at both marks when OK Labs opposed the registration of KOA's mark. After reviewing tons of documents, TTAB decided that the visual similarities were too close for comfort and sided with OK Labs and disallowed the "encircled half-moon K" mark from getting registered.

But KOA wasn't ready to throw in the towel! Despite TTAB's ruling, KOA kept using the "encircled half-moon k" mark. This led OK Labs to march into federal court, seeking an injunction to halt KOA's use of the confusingly similar mark. Initially, the court agreed with OK Labs, issuing the injunction based on the TTAB's findings.

However, the plot thickened! The case got sent back for a re-evaluation because the TTAB hadn't fully considered the broader marketplace context.

It turns out, determining whether consumers would confuse the two marks isn't just about how they look in isolation—it's also about how they're used in the bustling bazaar of kosher products.

The battles continued on, with Donel Corp (who took over OK Labs' "Circle-K" mark) getting an order that enjoined KOA from using its "encircled half-moon k" mark, its Disk-K Mark, or any other configuration or depiction of any letter K in any circle or circular disk!

In the end, this trademark tale underscores how crucial it is to look at the whole picture—because in the world of kosher certification, even the smallest mark can make a big difference.

Spark Networks (Jdate)
v.
Smooch Labs (JSwipe)

v.

Background

Spark Networks USA is a trailblazer in Jewish dating services. Since 1997, it has been a beacon for Jewish singles looking for love. The company proudly holds trademarks for its iconic "Jdate" logo and name. Enter 2014, and JSwipe (owned by Smooch Labs) makes its debut on the mobile dating scene, also catering to Jewish singles.

However, JSwipe's interface and branding bore a striking resemblance to Jdate's, perhaps causing a mix-up among users who couldn't tell if the two were related. (The specific logos above were NOT the issue in the trademark dispute, only the names).

Legal Dispute

Spark Networks' (Jdate's) Argument: Spark Networks claimed that JSwipe's use of the "J" prefix and its overall look were too similar to Jdate's trademarks. Spark Networks argued that this likeness misled users into thinking JSwipe was affiliated with or endorsed by Jdate. This, they said, amounted to trademark infringement. They sought an injunction to stop JSwipe from using its branding, and demanded damages for the infringement.

Smooch Labs' (JSwipe's) Arguments: Smooch Labs countered that the "J" prefix was generic when it came to Jewish-related services. They argued that "JSwipe" aptly described their app's purpose and that their branding was sufficiently different to avoid confusion. Additionally, they emphasized the different platforms (Jdate's website vs. JSwipe's mobile app) and user interfaces to bolster their argument against the likelihood of confusion.

Outcome

In 2015, the parties reached a settlement when Spark Networks (Jdate) acquired Smooch Labs (JSwipe). This acquisition allowed JSwipe to continue operating under Spark Networks' umbrella, effectively resolving the trademark dispute. The deal enabled Spark Networks to integrate JSwipe's user base and technology into its portfolio, combining the strengths of both brands.

Lessons to Be Learned:

1. **Trademark Protection in Niche Markets:** This case highlights the need for robust trademark protection, even in niche markets like religious dating services. Companies must protect their brand identity to maintain a competitive edge and prevent consumer confusion.
2. **Likelihood of Confusion:** The core issue in trademark infringement cases is the likelihood of consumer confusion. Distinct and clear branding is essential to prevent misleading the public about potential affiliations or endorsements.
3. **Strategic Resolutions:** Resolving trademark disputes through acquisition or strategic agreements can be an effective way to settle conflicts and leverage the strengths of competing brands.

The Jdate v. JSwipe case is a prime example of how trademark law plays out in the realm of online dating services, emphasizing the importance of maintaining clear and distinct branding to protect a company's identity and reputation.

Jews for Jesus v. Brodsky

Background

This book does not attempt to resolve the question of what counts as "Jewish." There is a controversial group called *Jews for Jesus*, known for their proselytizing efforts in spreading their religious message that Jews can remain Jews, and also believe in the divinity of Jesus Christ.

Jews for Jesus was cruising the Internet, when they stumbled upon a website run by one Steven Brodsky. To their dismay, Brodsky had registered the domain name "jewsforjesus.org" and was using it to post content that was, let's say, not exactly aligning with the views of *Jews for Jesus*. Feeling like their online identity had been hijacked, they decided to take action.

Legal Dispute

Jews for Jesus claimed that Brodsky's actions constituted both trademark infringement and cybersquatting. They argued that their organization's name was a registered trademark and that Brodsky's use of it was likely to confuse internet users.

Moreover, they claimed Brodsky had registered the domain name in bad faith, purely to disrupt their mission and direct traffic away from their official site.

Brodsky, on the other hand, countered that he had every right to use the domain name. He argued that his use was a form of free speech and that he wasn't attempting to confuse anyone but rather to express his own views about the group. He saw the case as a classic David vs. Goliath battle, fighting against what he perceived as an overreach by the larger organization.

Outcome

In a plot twist worthy of a cyber-thriller, the court ruled in favor of *Jews for Jesus*. They found that Brodsky's use of the domain name did indeed constitute trademark infringement and cybersquatting. The court decided that Brodsky's actions were likely to confuse visitors into thinking his site was affiliated with or endorsed by *Jews for Jesus*. As a result, Brodsky was ordered to hand over the domain name *to Jews for Jesus*, ensuring that their online identity remained intact and uncontested.

Moral of the Story

1. **Guard Your Digital Identity:** Just as you'd protect your physical property, keep a vigilant eye on your digital assets to prevent hijacking.
2. **Trademark Protection:** Ensure your trademarks are registered and defended, especially in the wild world of the Internet.
3. **Beware of Cybersquatting:** Register your domain names early to avoid landing in a cybersquatting conundrum.
4. **Free Speech vs. Infringement:** Understand the fine line between free speech and trademark infringement to navigate digital disputes effectively.

This legal tale serves as a reminder of the importance of maintaining control over your online presence. It highlights the challenges organizations face in the digital realm and the critical role of the courts in protecting trademarks and combating cybersquatting.

Kabbalah Yoga Inc. v. Audi Gozlan

Background

Kabbalah (and its various spellings) are the mystical and esoteric teachings of Judaism. Picture a tranquil yoga studio where the soft hum of meditation music mingles with the scent of lavender incense. Now, imagine that serenity being punctuated by a flurry of legal papers and the stern demeanor of a judge. Kabbalah Yoga Inc., hailing from sunny Florida, found themselves in a spiritual and legal conundrum. They discovered that Audi Gozlan, a yoga enthusiast from Canada, had registered several trademarks under "Kabalah Yoga." Gozlan used these trademarks for his unique blend of yoga instruction and mystical Kabbalistic teachings.

Legal Dispute

Kabbalah Yoga Inc. argued that they had first dibs on the "Kabbalah Yoga" name, having used it well before Gozlan. They claimed that Gozlan's use of the name was like trying to teach a downward dog to a cat—confusing and problematic. They wanted the court to cancel Gozlan's trademarks to protect their brand and prevent any more yogic mix-ups.

Gozlan countered with zen-like calm, arguing that his trademark registrations were legit. He maintained that there was no prior use by Kabbalah Yoga Inc. that could trump his own claims. Gozlan believed his trademarks were as distinct as different yoga poses, not confusing at all.

The Outcome

The Trademark Trial and Appeal Board (TTAB) rolled out their metaphorical yoga mats and dug into the evidence. They examined who had been doing the "Kabbalah Yoga" asanas first and whether Gozlan's use was likely to tie consumers into a confused knot. They compared marketing materials, timelines, and the overall consumer vibe surrounding the "Kabbalah Yoga" name.

In a twist more surprising than a well-executed crow pose, TTAB ruled in favor of Audi Gozlan. They concluded that Kabbalah Yoga Inc. failed to prove its claims of prior use and that Gozlan's trademarks did not create a likelihood of confusion. As a result, Gozlan retained his trademark registrations for "Kabalah Yoga."

Chapter 10
Muslim Trademark Disputes

Islam is a monotheistic religion that began in the 7th century in Mecca, a city in modern-day Saudi Arabia. It was founded by the Prophet Muhammad, who is considered the last prophet in a long line that includes figures like Abraham, Moses, and Jesus. Muslims, the followers of Islam, believe in one God, known in Arabic as Allah. The Quran, the holy book of Islam, is considered the literal word of God as revealed to Muhammad. It serves as a guide for how Muslims should live their lives, emphasizing values like compassion, justice, and community.

At its heart, Islam is about connecting with the divine through acts of worship and good deeds. Five pillars define the core practices: declaring faith in Allah and Muhammad, praying five times a day, giving to charity, fasting during the month of Ramadan, and making a pilgrimage to Mecca at least once in a lifetime if possible.

There been many trademark disputes amongst Muslim groups. One such type of dispute is use of the word "halal" within a business name. What does halal mean? Halal is an Arabic word that means "permissible" or "lawful." In the context of food, it means that the food and drinks are allowed according to Islamic law, analogous to what kosher is in Judaism. Halal rules do not allow the eating of pork (and some other animals), no alcohol, and has rules regarding the slaughtering method for animals.

The Halal Guys v. The Halal Girls

Background

In the bustling world of New York City street food, there was a legendary food cart that grew into a mighty franchise known as The Halal Guys. Starting in the 1990s, The Halal Guys expanded from a humble cart to an international chain, famous for their delicious gyro and chicken dishes. They even secured multiple federal trademark registrations, including "The Halal Guys" and their eye-catching logo, "The Halal Guys Gyro & Chicken."

Meanwhile, on Long Island, a new halal food business sprouted up, calling themselves The Halal Girls. The Halal Girls aimed to carve out their own niche in the halal food market. However, The Halal Guys soon discovered that The Halal Girls were using a name and branding that looked a bit too familiar, sparking concerns of potential consumer confusion.

Legal Dispute

The Halal Guys, feeling like their well-earned reputation was under threat, argued that The Halal Girls' similar name and logo amounted to trademark infringement and false designation of origin. They claimed that consumers might be misled into thinking there was a connection between the two businesses, giving The Halal Girls an unfair advantage.

Seeking to protect their brand, The Halal Guys asked for an injunction to stop The Halal Girls from using the contested name and branding, and also demanded damages.

On the other side, The Halal Girls contended that "halal" is a generic and descriptive term, making it tricky to monopolize. While they initially agreed to change their name after The Halal Guys' request, they continued to use similar branding and expanded their online presence. They argued that their efforts to rebrand were sufficient and insisted there was no intention to mislead consumers or infringe on The Halal Guys' trademarks.

Legal Outcome

The Halal Guys took their case to the Eastern District of New York in March 2021, asserting federal and state law claims. The court sided with The Halal Guys, agreeing that The Halal Girls' similar name and logo were likely to confuse consumers. Consequently, the court issued an injunction, requiring The Halal Girls to stop using the infringing name and branding. This meant The Halal Girls had to rebrand their restaurant and online presence to comply with the court's order.

Moral of the Story

1. **Importance of Trademark Protection:** Businesses, especially in the competitive food industry, must vigilantly protect their trademarks to prevent unauthorized use that could dilute their brand.
2. **Generic vs. Descriptive Terms:** While "halal" is a descriptive term, combining it with "Guys" and specific branding elements created a distinct and protectable trademark for The Halal Guys.
3. **Consumer Confusion:** The key issue in trademark infringement cases is the likelihood of consumer

confusion. Clear and distinct branding is essential to avoid misleading consumers.
4. **Legal Preparedness:** Smaller businesses must be ready for the legal and financial challenges of defending their branding, particularly when up against larger, well-established competitors.

This legal tale highlights the complexities of trademark law, especially regarding culturally significant terms like "halal." It underscores the importance of maintaining clear and distinct branding to protect business interests and consumer trust.

Match Group v. Muzmatch

Background

In the lively realm of dating apps, a notable legal skirmish involved the American heavyweight Match Group, owner of Tinder and Hinge, and the British startup Muzmatch, which caters to the Muslim community. This dispute, unfolded in the UK's Intellectual Property and Enterprise Court in late 2021, revolved around the use of the word "Match" in the Muzmatch brand.

Legal Dispute

Match Group's Claim: Match Group argued that Muzmatch's name could confuse customers into thinking there was an association between the two brands, suggesting that Muzmatch was capitalizing on Match Group's established reputation and investment.

Muzmatch's Defense: Muzmatch countered by saying the term "match" is a generic word commonly used in dating services and should not be monopolized by one entity. They insisted that their use of the word was merely descriptive of their matchmaking service, not an attempt to infringe on Match Group's brand.

Outcome

In April 2022, the court decided in favor of Match Group. The judgment concluded that Muzmatch had benefited from the established reputation of Match Group's trademarks and that there was a likely risk of confusion among consumers. As a result, Muzmatch rebranded to Muzz and launched a rebranded app in 2022.

Lessons to Be Learned

1. **Importance of Distinct Branding**: New companies should ensure that their branding is unique and does not infringe on existing trademarks to avoid legal entanglements.
2. **Trademark Vigilance**: It's vital for established companies to continuously monitor and protect their trademarks to safeguard their brand integrity and prevent dilution.
3. **Legal and Financial Preparedness**: Smaller companies must be prepared for the legal and financial challenges of defending against trademark infringement claims, especially when up against larger entities with extensive resources.

This case underscores the critical balance between protecting brand identity and allowing the fair use of common descriptive terms within industry sectors.

Chapter 11
Christian Trademark Disputes

This book isn't here to debate theology or decide who's a "real" Christian. Just like how we covered "Jews for Jesus v. Brodsky" in the "Jewish" chapter, we know some folks might get riled up about which groups are included here. If a group considers Jesus Christ a divine figure, they're in! This means The Church of Jesus Christ of Latter-day Saints (Mormon), Seventh Day Adventists, The Unification Church, Christian Science, and more! So, take a deep breath and enjoy the ride!

Can the Name of a Church or Faith Even be Protected?

Navigating the choppy waters of trademark law when it comes to religious group names can feel a bit like playing a heavenly game of "Hot or Not" with words. Consider the term "Mormon," for instance. Is it a generic term, as omnipresent as the stars in the sky, used broadly to describe anyone following a certain religious playbook? Or is it a specific marker, akin to a celestial sign, pointing directly to a single faith organization? The process of deciding whether a term like "Mormon" deserves trademark protection involves delving into a celestial knot of historical usage, cultural implications, and legal precedent.

The challenge here is quite unique. Religious terms often evolve into generic usage over time due to widespread adoption beyond their origins. For example, the term "Christian" originally denoted followers of Christ in a specific location but has become a generic term used globally across various denominations and sects. This widespread, generic usage makes it impossible that "Christian" could ever be trademarked, as it refers to a broad class of religious beliefs rather than a single source or entity.

On the other hand, specific religious terms that have not permeated into generic usage might qualify for trademark protection. For instance, "Scientology," a term coined by L. Ron Hubbard, is associated specifically with the Church of Scientology and is protected as a trademark (see the Scientology chapter). This is because the term does not describe a broad religious category but specifically refers to the teachings and practices of that particular organization.

Deciding if a religious term can be trademarked often boils down to how the term is perceived by the public: as a generic descriptor of religious beliefs or as an identifier linked to a specific group. This legal and linguistic balancing act involves not just lawyers but cultural scholars and linguists, making it a multidisciplinary dance around the nuances of language and law.

It's a high-stakes branding bingo where the calls are made in courtrooms and not church halls. The legal challenge is discerning whether a name is just part of the religious lingo or a divine identifier worthy of a trademark halo. Each case can set precedents that affect not just the organizations involved but also how the public perceives and interacts with these terms. Thus, the stakes are not just about legal rights but also about cultural and religious identity.

The Church of Jesus Christ of Latter-day Saints

What is the Church of Jesus Christ of Latter-day Saints?

The Church of Jesus Christ of Latter-day Saints, often known as the LDS Church or Mormon Church, is a global faith community with a focus on family, service, and a deep belief in Jesus Christ. Founded in the early 19th century by Joseph Smith, who is considered a prophet by Church members. The LDS Church centers its teachings on the Bible and the Book of Mormon, which details Jesus's visit to the Americas after his resurrection. It is this additional testament that sets them apart from other Christian denominations.

What Names Should be Used When Describing Members of the Church of Jesus Christ of Latter-day Saints?

According to The Church of Jesus Christ of Latter-day Saints official style guide, it is most respectful and accurate to use the full name of the Church. While the terms "Mormons" and "LDS" have been widely used, the Church leadership has encouraged the use of the Church's full name to avoid misconceptions and to highlight their commitment to Christ.

When a shorter reference is needed, "Latter-day Saints" is an appropriate and respectful term.

Why So Much Emphasis on Naming this Group in this Book?

If you've learned anything so far, it's that words and names matter! Ironically, despite trying to steer away people from referring to their religion and members as "Mormon," The Church of Jesus Christ of Latter-day Saints has spent a lot of resources preventing others from using that term for various goods and services.

The LDS Church and Trademark Law

The LDS Church has registered many trademarks to safeguard its name, symbols, and related terminology. These trademarks help keep the church's identity intact and ensure its religious materials, services, and events are not misrepresented. The Church's trademarks cover a variety of categories, including religious services, educational services, printed materials, and online content. However, whether using the word "Mormon" is allowed is a grey area, as we will see from the cases below.

Intellectual Reserve, Inc. v. Sheets (Mormon v. Secret Mormon)

Background

In 2007, a creative soul named Kendal Sheets decided to trademark the catchy phrase "Secret Mormon" for products such as books, magazines, and newsletters, all revolving around historical and fictional religious events. Initially, the trademark examiner gave it a thumbs-up, and thought there were no conflicting trademarks in sight.

Legal Dispute

However, this tale took a twist when Intellectual Reserve, Inc., the guardians of all trademark things Latter-day Saint related, filed an opposition with the Trademark Trial and Appeal Board (TTAB). Intellectual Reserve pointed out their treasure trove of trademarks featuring the word "Mormon," like "Book of Mormon," "Mormon Tabernacle Choir," "Mormon.org," and "Mormon Handicraft." They argued that they owned the trademark rights to "Mormon" and that these trademarks were symbols of their goods and services associated with the Church. The fear was that people might get confused and think "Secret Mormon" was linked to the Church.

Sheets, on the other hand, argued that "Mormon" was a generic term. He pointed out that it wasn't distinctive and could refer to various denominations and sects, with only the largest being the Church of Jesus Christ of Latter-day Saints. He mentioned other groups like the Community of Christ (formerly known as the Reorganized Church of Jesus Christ of Latter Day saints), in Independence Missouri, or the Church of Jesus Christ of Latter Saints (Strangite) in Burlington, Wisconsin, or various Fundamentalist Mormon sects.

Sheets cited the Merriam-Webster's Encyclopedia of World Religions, which stated that a Mormon is "a member of any of several denominations and sects, the largest of which is the Church of Jesus Christ of Latter-Day Saints, that trace their origins to a religion founded by Joseph Smith in the United States about 1830." Not only did Sheets want a registration for "Secret Mormon," he also wanted the Trademark Office to cancel all of the Church's trademarks that had the word "Mormon" in it, claiming they were just "merely descriptive."

Outcome

In a twist of irony, even though the Church of Jesus Christ of Latter-day Saints doesn't favor the word "Mormon" to describe themselves, they are fiercely protective of it legally. While the case promised an intriguing showdown, Kendal Sheets eventually decided to withdraw his trademark application. Consequently, the Trademark Trial and Appeal Board closed the case without making any formal decision on the matter.

Eller v. Intellectual Reserve, Inc.
(Mormon Match v. The LDS Church)

MormonMatch

LatterDate

Background

Love was in the air, but so was a trademark dispute when Jonathan Eller set up the dating website "Mormon Match," registering the domain www.dateamormon.com, and attempting to register the name and logo "Mormon Match." Eller was trying to help singles in the Church of Jesus Christ of Latter-day Saints find their perfect matches. The Church, known for its keen sense of trademark guardianship, wasn't ready to let this matchmaking attempt slide by unnoticed.

Legal Dispute

The Church filed a lawsuit against Jonathan Eller, the founder of "Mormon Match," arguing that the use of "Mormon" might confuse the faithful into thinking that the dating site was Church-sanctioned, and also pointing out that the Church owned numerous trademark registrations that have the word "Mormon." Interestingly, previously, the Church tried to register the word "Mormon" for religious services and ministerial services, but was refused based on genericness. However, the Church was allowed to register the single word "Mormon" for specific goods and services, including "Educational services, namely, providing classes, conferences, and institutes in the fields of history and religion" and "genealogy services."

Eller pushed back, claiming that "Mormon," as the Trademark Office noted in its refusal for religious services, is a generic term, and therefore fair game for describing his site's intended audience. The case, infused with debates over religious freedom and intellectual property rights, captured the media's attention, turning a legal battle into a public spectacle.

Outcome

Before the courts could put their stamp on the case, both parties decided to settle out of the spotlight. The resolution? "Mormon Match" would go on a branding blind date, changing its name to "Latter Date" and ensuring its new identity steered clear of any ecclesiastical entanglements. The settlement emphasized respecting the Church's trademark rights, likely saving both sides from further heartache and legal fees. The Church noted that it would not object to using the word "Mormon" to describe the intended audience, such as "A dating sight for Mormons."

Lessons Learned

This case highlighted a few key takeaways for the lovelorn and the legally minded:

1. **Trademark Tango:** Religious organizations like the LDS Church will step up to protect their intellectual property, especially when it comes to terms that might imply endorsement.
2. **Descriptive Dilemmas:** Just because a term describes a community doesn't mean it's available for commercial love stories — especially if it's trademarked.
3. **Settlement Smooches:** Sometimes, reaching a mutual agreement is better than enduring a prolonged courtship with the legal system.

Moving Forward

The LDS Church continues to watch over its trademarks zealously, ensuring that terms like "The Church of Jesus Christ of Latter-day Saints," "Mormon Tabernacle Choir," and "Book of Mormon" are used appropriately. As for the rest of us, this tale serves as a reminder to tread carefully in the tricky terrain of trademarks in dating and beyond. Whether you're starting a business or a dating site, a little trademark research might just save you a big legal headache. Remember, in the world of trademarks and matchmaking, it's always best to look before you leap!

Intellectual Reserve, Inc.
v.
Heathertainment, Inc.

(Mormon v. Bad Mormon)

Background: The "Bad Mormon" Trademark Tangle

In a world where trademarks clash with TV stars, the dispute between The Church of Jesus Christ of Latter-day Saints and Heather Gay's Heathertainment, Inc. takes center stage. Let's unpack this legal drama that's as spicy as a reality TV plot twist! Heather Gay (one of the stars of the show of The Real Housewives of Salt Lake City), in true reality TV fashion, ventured into the trademark world with her applications to trademark "Bad Mormon," for various goods, a term she wanted to splash across beverage containers, clothing, and podcasts. This move was tied to her book release, intriguingly titled "Bad Mormon," released in 2023.

Legal Dispute

The LDS Church, not amused and perhaps lacking a sense of reality TV humor, opposed the trademark application. Their legal briefs were not short of drama. The Church argued that "Bad Mormon" might confuse the flock into thinking the Church had given its holy nod to Heather's merch. The sacred trademarks of the Church, they claimed, would be tarnished by association with the term. "Bad Mormon" could mislead the masses into thinking the Church had some sort of partnership with Heather's ventures.

Outcome

As the legal eagles prepared their arguments, the stage was set for a showdown at the Trademark Trial and Appeal Board (TTAB). In January of 2024, before TTAB could come to a decision, Heather Gay abandoned her trademark application for "Bad Mormon." Her book was released and it appears that all litigation regarding "Bad Mormon" has ceased.

Reflections and Revelations

1. **Trademark Protection:** Just like their temples, religious organizations zealously guard their trademarks. This case is a testament to their commitment to maintaining brand sanctity.
2. **Fair Use vs. Fame:** Heather's case highlights the tightrope walk between using descriptive terms associated with a religious group and stepping on trademark toes.
3. **The PR Plot:** With a reality star in the mix, the Church's aggressive trademark tactics could stir up more than just legal debates—it's a full-blown PR ballet.

Holy Spirit Association for the Unification of World Christianity
v.
World Peace and Unification Sanctuary, Inc.

"Will the Real Unification Church Please Stand Up!"

Background: The Twelve Gates Symbol Skirmish

In the tranquil but sometimes tumultuous world of religious movements, not all battles are spiritual—some end up in the courtroom, complete with gavels and legal briefs. The Holy Spirit Association for the Unification of World Christianity (known colloquially as the Unification Church) is a relatively new religious movement founded by Sun Myung Moon in 1954. Moon considered himself to be the Second Coming of Christ. Needless to say, this church has had its critics. The case of Holy Spirit Association for the Unification of World Christianity v. World Peace and Unification Sanctuary, Inc., also known as the Twelve Gates Symbol Skirmish, is one such tale of who owns the trademarks to this religious group.

The drama unfolded in the U.S. District Court for the Middle District of Pennsylvania in 2018. At the heart of this divine dispute was the Twelve Gates symbol, also known as the Tongil symbol, crafted by the late Reverend Sun Myung Moon back in 1965. Fast forward a few decades, and after the death of Sun Myung Moon, his son Sean Moon founded the Sanctuary Church, and started using this symbol on websites and during their eyebrow-raising "Rod of Iron" ministries (which mixed firearms with faith), and more.

Legal Dispute

The official body of the Unification Church wasn't pleased. They argued that the Sanctuary Church's liberal use of the Twelve Gates symbol was a classic case of trademark infringement and unfair competition under the Lanham Act. They worried that followers might get the wrong idea—that the Sanctuary Church was part of the official Unification family.

On the other side of the pew, the Sanctuary Church claimed they were just keeping it in the family, asserting that all assets, trademarks included, were theirs by divine right following Reverend Moon's departure to the heavenly realm. They argued that their use of the symbol was part and parcel of their religious practices and teachings. They also argued that the symbol is now generic, and just represents Unificationism generally, and not entitled to trademark protection at all anymore.

Outcome

The courtroom turned into a theological think tank as both sides presented arguments steeped in both law and spirituality. However, U.S. District Judge Jennifer P. Wilson decided to sit this dance out, invoking the "ecclesiastical abstention doctrine." She ruled that digging into this dispute would mean meddling in the murky waters of religious doctrine and church governance—areas where judges fear to tread.

What is the Ecclesiastical Abstention Doctrine?

Imagine you're at a big family reunion where everyone's debating whether Aunt Edna's secret recipe should include nuts or not. It's a family matter, deeply personal, and definitely not something you'd ask a stranger at the next table to weigh in on, right? Well, in the legal world, courts treat religious disputes much like our hypothetical family dilemma over Aunt Edna's recipe—with a respectful distance.

The "ecclesiastical abstention doctrine" is the court's way of saying, "This seems like a family issue, so you folks should probably figure it out yourselves." This principle comes from the recognition that civil courts are neither equipped nor authorized to delve into matters of religious doctrine, church governance, or spiritual practices. It's part of a broader legal stance known as "non-entanglement," which is all about keeping church and state in their respective corners to avoid a messy tug-of-war.

Non-entanglement takes this a step further by ensuring courts don't get tangled up in religious teachings or internal church disputes. Think of it as a polite refusal to RSVP to a religious debate. The idea here is to avoid any scenario where a judge ends up playing theologian, which could lead to inappropriate government interference in religious matters.

So, when a legal battle gets too heavenly (or doctrinal), the "ecclesiastical abstention doctrine" and non-entanglement principle act as the court's "no thank you" to diving into divine disputes. It's the legal equivalent of staying out of the kitchen during a family recipe feud, keeping the peace and letting spiritual matters simmer on their own.

When courts bump into issues covered by the "ecclesiastical abstention doctrine," they act much like a polite guest at a religious potluck who avoids meddling in the kitchen. Here's what they defer to, using a light touch and a respect for boundaries:

1. **Church Autonomy**: Imagine if every time you tried to set up the rules for your own house party, your neighbor insisted on telling you how to arrange the furniture. Not cool, right? Courts feel the same about stepping into religious organizations' internal matters. They respect that religious groups know best how to handle their own spiritual and organizational issues, and they keep their legal noses out of it.
2. **First Amendment Protections**: This is like the golden rule at a constitutional garden party. Just as you wouldn't want someone crashing your party and dictating the theme, courts avoid crashing religious gatherings with legal judgments. By stepping back, they honor everyone's right to religious freedom, ensuring that church affairs remain free from government interference.
3. **Religious Doctrine and Decisions**: Courts are wary of acting like uninvited judges at a doctrinal debate club. If a dispute requires picking apart religious beliefs or deciding who's right in matters of faith, courts prefer to RSVP with a polite "no thanks." They recognize that religious questions are best answered by those within the faith.
4. **Internal Church Governance**: It's a bit like not telling someone how to organize their family reunion. Whether it's choosing leaders or disciplining members, courts understand that religious organizations have their own rulebook. Interfering in these decisions would be like rearranging the family photo without being in it.

In essence, when it comes to matters covered by the ecclesiastical abstention doctrine, courts prefer to keep the peace by keeping their distance. They recognize that when it comes to religion, it's best to let the insiders handle the inner workings. This approach not only keeps the courts from getting tangled in theological thorns but also respects the essence of religious freedom.

The case was dismissed, not on the merits of the trademark claims, but because the court found itself grappling with questions better suited for a higher power (or at least a different venue). Judge Wilson's hands-off approach highlighted the delicate balance courts must maintain when earthly laws collide with heavenly decrees.

Lessons Learned: Keeping the Faith and the Peace

1. **Religious Trademark Disputes**: These can spiral into complex doctrinal debates, showing that not all legal battles are cut out for secular courts.
2. **Ecclesiastical Abstention Doctrine**: This legal principle serves as a reminder that there's a line courts will not cross, preserving the sanctity of religious governance.
3. **Clear Governance in Faith Organizations**: To avoid divine disputes, religious groups might consider setting in stone (or at least in some very clear bylaws) who holds the keys to the kingdom—of trademarks, that is.

In the grand celestial scheme of things, the Twelve Gates Symbol Skirmish teaches us that even in matters of faith, a little legal foresight and a lot of clear governance can prevent a whole lot of earthly entanglements. And for those navigating the nexus of law and spirituality, this case serves as a heavenly cautionary tale.

The Universal Church, Inc.
v.
Universal Life Church/ULC Monastery

"The Battle of Universality"

Background

In 2014, The Universal Church, based in New York, filed a lawsuit against the Universal Life Church/ULC Monastery, claiming trademark infringement over the use of "Universal Church." Universal Life Church had registered numerous domain names, used HTML metadata tags, and placed web advertisements for search results using "Universal Church." The defendant contended that the term was too generic to be trademarked and used broadly across various religious entities.

Legal Dispute

The Universal Church argued that their long-standing use and registration in 2006 of "Universal Church" granted them exclusive trademark rights, which were being violated by the Universal Life Church's similar use, causing confusion among the public. Universal Life Church/ULC Monastery countered that "universal" was a generic term used historically across many Christian denominations and could not be monopolized by any single entity. They argued that there was no likelihood of confusion because their services were distinctly different.

Outcome

The court's analysis focused on the genericness of the term "Universal Church." It examined historical and contemporary uses of the term, evaluating whether it had become generic through common use in religious contexts. The court also considered trademark principles such as the likelihood of confusion and the strength of the mark claimed by The Universal Church.

The court ruled in favor of the Universal Life Church/ULC Monastery, finding that "Universal Church" is a generic term that cannot be exclusively owned. It determined that there was no significant likelihood of confusion between the two organizations, given their different operational models and audiences. This decision highlighted the challenges in trademarking terms that have broad historical and communal use in religious contexts.

Seventh-Day Adventists v. McGill

Background

In the heavenly realm of trademark law, few cases get as spirited as the clash between the General Conference Corporation of Seventh-Day Adventists and Walter McGill. Let's dive into this celestial legal battle, which had more twists than a heavenly staircase!

The Seventh-Day Adventist Church, a well-established Christian denomination, found itself locking legal horns with Pastor Walter McGill, who boldly named his small congregation the "Creation Seventh Day Adventist Church." The official Seventh-Day Adventist Church was not amused, claiming McGill was infringing on their heavenly trademark.

Legal Dispute

The General Conference argued that they had a trademark on "Seventh-Day Adventist," and McGill's use was creating confusion among the earthly and possibly celestial beings alike, diluting the holy brand. They contended that trademark rights trumped McGill's First Amendment rights in this scenario because preventing confusion is a higher calling.

McGill claimed that using "Seventh-Day Adventist" was a matter of religious identity and expression, deeply rooted in First Amendment protections. McGill stood his ground with religious conviction, invoking the Religious Freedom

Restoration Act (RFRA) as a shield, arguing that faith should trump commerce. He also argued that the term "Seventh-Day Adventist" had become generic, used widely beyond the confines of the trademark, much like people use "Kleenex" for any tissue.

Outcome

The court had to ponder whether the Seventh-Day Adventist trademark could restrict religious expression. Was McGill's small congregation stepping on divine trademarks, or merely exercising their spiritual and speech freedoms?

Could a religious designation become so common that it loses its trademark protection, floating freely like clouds in the public domain? This was a key question for the court to decide, balancing trademark protections against the generic use of religious terms.

The court ultimately sided with the General Conference, ruling that the trademark "Seventh-Day Adventist" was not generic and deserved protection from unauthorized heavenly uses. McGill's argument that the term was a generic descriptor of faith did not sway the celestial scales of justice.

The court delicately balanced the First Amendment rights, concluding that protecting the public from confusion about religious affiliations outweighed McGill's right to use the trademarked name in his church's title.

Lessons Learned

1. **Trademark Sanctity:** Even in the realms of faith, trademarks hold a sacred spot. Religious organizations can protect their names from unauthorized earthly uses that might mislead the flock.
2. **First Amendment Limits:** While freedom of speech and religion are celestial rights, they orbit around the gravitational pull of trademark laws designed to prevent public confusion.

3. **The Genericism Galaxy:** Proving that a religious term has become generic is as tough as turning water into wine. It requires showing widespread usage beyond the trademark owner's control.

First Church of Christ, Scientist v. Evans

Background

In the celestial courtrooms where legal minds and divine doctrines converge, the case of the General Conference Corp. of Christian Science Board of Directors of the First Church of Christ, Scientist v. Evans shines a light on the intricate dance between trademark law and religious expressions. Let's unpack this heavenly debate with a sprinkle of lightheartedness and some divine intervention!

The drama unfolded when The First Church of Christ, Scientist (also known as the Mother Church), based in the sacred grounds of Boston, Massachusetts, found itself at odds with a former member and his breakaway faction. This renegade group dared to use the "Christian Science" moniker after parting ways with the main congregation. Heaven forbid! The dispute centered around whether this celestial name could be trademarked and kept exclusive to the original denominational entity.

Legal Dispute

The Mother Church argued that "Christian Science" wasn't just any old name — it had evolved to signify more than just a religious practice. With its hallowed services and divine publications, the name had, they claimed, ascended to a higher realm of trademark protection under the Lanham Act.

The defendants countered with a proclamation that "Christian Science" was as generic as manna from heaven—a term for the religion itself that couldn't be claimed by any single faction of the faithful.

Outcome

The New Jersey Supreme Court, in its analysis, pointed out that while the Mother Church had a long-standing association with the term, it primarily denoted a religious practice rather than a source of goods or services. As such, the term was ruled generic and not subject to trademark protection. The court found that preventing others from using "Christian Science" in their church names would unjustly restrict religious expression and access to the public domain.

With a gavel strike that might have echoed through the heavens, the court dismissed the Mother Church's earthly claims, allowing the breakaway group to continue their spiritual journey under the "Christian Science" banner. The courts decreed that such a universally used term for a belief system was beyond the reach of trademark constraints.

Lessons Learned

1. **Heavenly Boundaries of Trademark Law**: This celestial case underscores the complexities when heavenly names meet earthly laws. For religious entities seeking trademark protection, there's a high bar to prove that religious terms have morphed into distinctive commercial identifiers.
2. **Freedom of Faithful Expressions**: The ruling reinforced the sacred principle that religious terms, used broadly to describe doctrines and beliefs, should roam free, unshackled by commercial monopolies.
3. **Moral of the Story**: For religious groups, the path to trademarking a name is strewn with both legal and ethical considerations. It's a journey that requires

navigating not just the narrow gates of trademark law but also the broader avenues of religious freedom and expression.

In the grand cosmic scheme of things, the case of "Christian Science" serves as a divine guidepost, illuminating the delicate balance between protecting a church's identity and ensuring that expressions of faith remain as free as the heavenly spirits they evoke. For those walking the line between the sacred and the legal, this case is a testament to the principle that in matters of faith, sometimes, letting go is just as powerful as holding on.

Archdiocese of St. Louis
v.
Internet Entertainment Group (IEG), Inc.

Background

The Archdiocese of St. Louis was eagerly preparing for Pope John Paul II's visit to the United States in 1999. They registered a bunch of trademarks in July 1998 to promote the event, wanting to showcase the spiritual significance and spread positive vibes about the Pope's visit. Meanwhile, Internet Entertainment Group (IEG), a company famous for its adult entertainment websites, decided to register two domain names: "papalvisit.com" and "papalvisit1999.com." These sites weren't just about the Pope's visit, they also featured some spicy content and jokes about the Pope and the Roman Catholic Church.

Legal Dispute

The Archdiocese wasn't amused by IEG's antics. They filed a lawsuit accusing IEG of trademark infringement, trademark dilution, false designation of origin, and unfair competition. They wanted the court to issue a temporary restraining order (TRO) and a preliminary injunction to stop

IEG from using those domain names and anything similar to their "Papal Visit 1999" trademarks.

IEG, on the other hand, claimed they were simply exercising their right to free speech under the First Amendment. They argued that their domain names were generic and that their use was a form of free expression, which shouldn't be restricted.

Outcome

The court had to first figure out if it even had the right to hear this case. They applied the Missouri Long-Arm Statute and the Federal Trademark Dilution Act (FTDA) and found that IEG's websites, with all their enticing hyperlinks, were actively encouraging web users to click around. This was enough for the court to claim jurisdiction.

The court then zoomed in on the main issue: whether IEG's use of the domain names and their explicit content amounted to trademark infringement and dilution. They concluded that the use of pornographic material under these domain names indeed infringed on the Archdiocese's trademark rights and tarnished the marks.

IEG's defense didn't hold up. The court clarified that this wasn't a free speech issue but rather a trademark misuse issue. They found that IEG's actions led to consumer confusion and damaged the image linked to the Archdiocese's marks.

The court emphasized that IEG's actions were completely at odds with the spiritual and positive image the Archdiocese wanted to promote with the Pope's visit. This ruling highlighted the importance of protecting trademark rights and preserving the integrity of culturally and spiritually significant events.

The case of Archdiocese of St. Louis v. Internet Entertainment Group is a prime example of how trademark law can intersect with cultural sensitivity and Internet commerce. It underscores the need to respect religious and cultural symbols in the digital age and ensure they aren't exploited for commercial gain in ways that undermine their intended significance.

Chapter 12
Scientology Trademark Disputes

Scientology is the brainchild of L. Ron Hubbard and started as a self-help program called Dianetics. After a rocky start, Hubbard pivoted, relaunching his ideas as a religion—and thus, Scientology was born. By 1954, Hubbard was back in the saddle with the rights to Dianetics and the Church of Scientology was established, becoming the main hub for all things Scientology, although a rebel group called the Free Zone also practices independently.

Scientology's belief system includes ideas like reincarnation and the concept that minds are have "engrams," or traumatic memories, that only a process called "auditing" can clear. Once cleared of these engrams, followers achieve "clear" status and can move up realms of Operating Thetan levels, which are as secretive as they are expensive.

Despite the hush-hush nature, the juicy details of these levels, have found their way onto the Internet, courtesy of sites like WikiLeaks.

Scientology is known for being very aggressive with protecting their intellectual property rights, so to call Scientology a controversial organization would be an understatement. Many of the Scientology lawsuits are more about copyright infringement, where an individual or group has taken the writings of Scientology and L. Ron Hubbard, and posted them on the Internet to criticize Scientology. While Scientology owns many trademarks, the trademarks disputes are usually secondary to their copyright infringement disputes.

The purpose of the book (and this chapter) is to highlight interesting trademark disputes that have arisen with religious and spiritual groups, not to comment on substantively on any belief system.

Religious Technology Center
v.
Freie Zone E. V

Background

In the realm of domain name disputes, we delve into the quirky arbitration case between the Religious Technology Center (RTC) and Freie Zone E.V, overseen by The WIPO (World Intellectual Property Organization) Arbitration and Mediation Center. This digital drama revolves around the contentious domain name scientologie.org.

Legal Dispute

The Religious Technology Center (RTC), an organization based in California. RTC is responsible for managing all intellectual property related to Scientology, originally developed by L. Ron Hubbard. Freie Zone e.V., also known as the Free Zone Association, is a German group that promotes the free use of L. Ron Hubbard's philosophies.

The focal point of the dispute was the domain name scientologie.org, registered with Network Solutions, Inc. (NSI). RTC initiated the complaint on May 9, 2000, which led to the involvement of WIPO. The process included multiple submissions from both parties.

RTC argued that scientologie.org was virtually identical or confusingly similar to their trademarks, such as SCIENTOLOGIE and SCIENTOLOGY. RTC claimed that Freie Zone had no legitimate reason to own the domain name. RTC accused Freie Zone of registering the domain in bad faith, intending to mislead and confuse users.

Freie Zone contended that the domain was used to promote a 1934 book by Dr. Anastasius Nordenholz, titled "Scientologie - Wissenschaft von der Beschaffenheit und Tauglichkeit des Wissens (Scientology: Science of the

Constitution and Usefulness of Knowledge)." They asserted their intentions were sincere, aimed at spreading philosophical knowledge rather than causing confusion.

Freie Zone emphasized their independence from both the Church of Scientology and RTC, striving to avoid any misconceptions.

Outcome

The Panelist agreed that scientologie.org was strikingly similar to RTC's trademarks, which posed a potential issue. However, the Panelist found that Freie Zone had legitimate reasons for owning the domain. Their rights to promote Dr. Nordenholz's book, which predated RTC's trademarks, were deemed valid and reasonable.

RTC's argument fell short. The Panelist did not find sufficient evidence to support the claim that Freie Zone registered the domain in bad faith. Given Freie Zone's legitimate interests, the bad faith claim was not upheld.

The decision favored Freie Zone. RTC's request to transfer the domain name was denied, allowing Freie Zone to continue using scientologie.org for their philosophical endeavors.

Lessons Learned

1. **Evidence of Bad Faith:** Demonstrating bad faith requires substantial proof, which RTC lacked in this case.
2. **Role of Historical Rights:** Historical rights, such as those to Dr. Nordenholz's work, can significantly influence the outcome of legal disputes.
3. **Arbitration Process:** Engaged and thorough participation by both parties resulted in a well-rounded and fair decision.

The Church of Scientology
v.
Elmira Mission

Background:

In 1975, the Elmira Mission decided to get cozy with the Church of Scientology, officially becoming part of the group and earning the right to use all the Scientology trademarks. In return, they agreed to send 10% of their income back to the Church as a kind of spiritual subscription fee. A few years later, in 1981, the Church decided to shuffle things around and handed over all its trademark rights to a new organization called the Religious Technology Center (RTC). RTC quickly upped the price tag, and by 1982, the Elmira Mission was now on the hook for 15% of its income, plus some extra fees, just to keep using those valuable trademarks.

Legal Dispute

Things were smooth sailing until November 1984, when Palmer, the head of the Elmira Mission, decided to stop paying those fees altogether. The Church of Scientology, not one to let that slide, took Palmer and the Mission to court, accusing them of trademark infringement. The Church's argument was simple: "If you want to keep using our stuff, you've got to pay up!"

Outcome

The court agreed with The Church of Scientology, seeing that the Elmira Mission couldn't just keep using the trademarks without holding up their end of the deal, proving that the Elmira Mission had indeed been playing fast and loose with the rules. The details of how things were settled remain a mystery, as the court decided to seal that part of the story, leaving everyone guessing about the final outcome. But one thing's for sure—Palmer learned the hard way that you can't skip out on your trademark dues! Later, Palmer developed his own spiritual and self-help system, having some similarities to Scientology, and called it The Avatar Course (logo above).

Chapter 13
Hindu and Buddhist Trademark Disputes

Hinduism is like a grand tapestry of beliefs and practices, with a bit of something for everyone. At its core, Hindus believe in a supreme being called Brahma, who is the source of everything in the universe. But instead of one single form, Brahma is seen in many different ways, through gods and goddesses like Vishnu, Shiva, and Lakshmi, each with their own special roles and stories.

Hindus also believe in karma, which means that every action has consequences, and reincarnation, where the soul is reborn in a new body until it finally reaches liberation, or moksha. It's a journey that can take many lifetimes, but there's no rush—the universe is patient!

Buddhism is like a practical guide to living a peaceful and mindful life. Founded by Siddhartha Gautama, who became known as the Buddha, it focuses on the idea that life is full of suffering, but there's a way to end that suffering by following the Eightfold Path. This path is all about right actions, thoughts, and intentions—basically, being a good person and staying aware of your mind and surroundings. Buddhists believe in the concept of nirvana, which is the ultimate goal of breaking free from the cycle of birth and rebirth, reaching a state of complete peace and enlightenment. It's a path anyone can follow, with the Buddha's teachings lighting the way.

What ties all these beliefs and practices together is the idea of a journey—whether it's the Hindu path to moksha, or the Buddhist pursuit of nirvana. Each one offers a unique perspective on life, the universe, and everything in between, but they all share a common goal: to help people find peace, happiness, and a deeper understanding of themselves and the world around them. So whether you're chanting a mantra, meditating under a Bodhi tree, or just trying to nail that tricky yoga pose, you're part of a rich tradition that's been guiding people on their spiritual journeys for thousands of years.

However, just like any good family dinner, things also get spicy when sects start arguing over who gets to use the sacred symbols! So, buckle up and grab some popcorn because we're about to dive into the wild world of trademark disputes that are anything but Zen!

Self-Realization Fellowship Church
v.
Ananda Church of Self-Realization

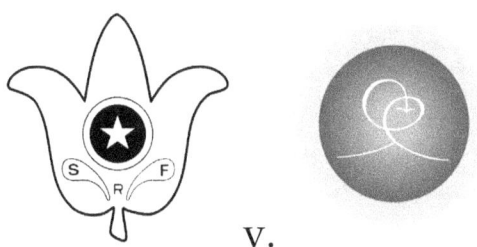

v.

Background

The legal skirmish between the Self-Realization Fellowship Church (SRFC) and the Ananda Church of Self-Realization (Ananda) was not your typical trademark tussle. Both organizations dedicated themselves to promoting the teachings of Paramahansa Yogananda, a revered spiritual leader. The Ananda Church of Self-Realization was founded by a former disciple of Yogananda named Swami Kriyananda. Kriyananda left SRFC and started his own community based on Yogananda's teachings. The controversy arose when SRFC accused Ananda of trademark infringement for their similarly inspired name.

Legal Dispute

SRFC claimed exclusive rights to the term "Self-Realization," arguing it was synonymous with their spiritual teachings and services, which had been in use long before ACSR's establishment. They contended that Anand's "Self-Realization" name could easily mislead devotees and spiritual seekers into believing that Ananda was affiliated or endorsed by SRFC, diluting their established brand.

Ananda argued that "Self-Realization" was a generic term used widely in spiritual contexts, thus not subject to trademark protection. They claimed that their use of the term was in good faith, intended to honor Yogananda's teachings, not to confuse the public or capitalize on SRFC's reputation.

Outcome

The crux of the legal debate hinged on whether "Self-Realization" had become indistinguishable from the spiritual teachings of SRFC or if it remained a generic term usable by any organization promoting Yogananda's methods. The court also delved into trademark law's nuances, examining the balance between protecting established names and allowing the use of common spiritual terms.

After a 12-year-long legal battle, the court ruled in favor of the Ananda Church of Self-Realization. The decision emphasized several critical points:

1. **Generic Term Ruling**: The term "Self-Realization" could not be trademarked by SRF because it was a generic term widely used in spiritual contexts.
2. **Public Domain**: The name "Paramahansa Yogananda" and other related terms and images could not be exclusively owned under trademark law as they were either generic or had become part of the public domain.
3. **No Infringement**: Ananda's use of these terms did not infringe on any protectable trademark rights held by SRF.
4. **No Deception**: Ananda was not found to be trying to mislead or confuse the public into thinking it was part of or endorsed by SRFC.

This case highlighted the limits of intellectual property rights within spiritual and religious contexts, establishing that names of historical spiritual figures and generic spiritual terms often cannot be exclusively controlled by any one organization.

Dogfish Head Brewery v. Whip In

The Namaste Brew Brawl

Background

In the vibrant world of craft beer, where creativity and tradition blend harmoniously, a trademark dispute between two breweries over the name "Namaste" emerged, sparking a lively debate about culture, branding, and the spirit of collaboration.

Whip In, a South Austin establishment known for its Indian fusion cuisine and craft beers, decided to name one of its creations "Namaste." However, Dogfish Head Brewery, a well-established craft brewery from Delaware, had already trademarked "Namaste" for its popular witbier. This led to a trademark conflict that forced Whip In to reconsider its beer's name.

Legal Dispute

Dogfish Head had trademarked "Namaste" for their witbier and argued that it needed to protect its brand to avoid consumer confusion and maintain their market identity.

Under trademark law, Dogfish Head had a legitimate claim to protect its brand identity and prevent market confusion. Their prior use and established reputation with "Namaste" gave them a strong legal standing.

Whip In contended that "Namaste" is a common term in Indian culture, symbolizing peace and respect, and should not be restricted by trademark. They argued that the name was chosen to reflect the cultural roots and spirit of their beer.

The trademark dispute centers around the principles of trademark law, which aims to prevent consumer confusion and protect established brands. However, it also raised questions about cultural appropriation and the extent to which common cultural terms should be trademarked.

The use of "Namaste," a term deeply rooted in Indian culture, highlighted the tension between cultural heritage and commercial interests. Whip In's argument brought attention to the broader implications of trademarking culturally significant terms.

Outcome

Ultimately, Whip In agreed to change the name of their beer from "Namaste" to "Kamala," which means lotus flower in Hindi. This resolution allowed Dogfish Head to maintain its trademark while enabling Whip In to honor its cultural roots with a new, meaningful name.

The Namaste beer trademark dispute serves as a reminder of the complexities inherent in balancing legal protections, cultural respect, and commercial interests. It highlights the importance of due diligence in branding and the need for sensitivity when dealing with culturally significant terms. In the end, the resolution fostered a spirit of cooperation and respect, allowing both breweries to continue their creative endeavors in the ever-evolving world of craft beer.

The International Society of Consciousness (ISKCON)
v.
ISKCON Apparel

Factual Background

Imagine, if you will, a serene temple where the chants of "Hare Krishna, Hare Krishna" float through the air, mingling with the scent of incense. Devotees, clad in flowing robes, bow in reverence to statues of Krishna, their hearts filled with devotion. Now, juxtapose this peaceful scene with the chaotic hustle of a courtroom, where lawyers in crisp suits battle over the sacred letters "ISKCON."

The International Society for Krishna Consciousness (ISKCON), or the Hare Krishnas as they are more popularly known, has been a beacon of spirituality and devotion since its founding by A.C. Bhaktivedanta Swami Prabhupada in New York City back in 1966. From its humble beginnings, ISKCON has grown into a global movement, spreading the teachings of Krishna and the Bhagavad Gita far and wide.

Along with its spiritual outreach, ISKCON has also become synonymous with its distinctive branding – a trademark that symbolizes a global family bound by faith and devotion.

In February 2020, some sharp-eyed devotees conducting routine Internet research stumbled upon the "ISKCON Apparel" website. They were shocked to find that this company was boldly using the ISKCON trademark to sell their products. These weren't just your everyday knock-offs; the brand was unapologetically splashing the sacred acronym on everything from hoodies to handbags. For the devout members of ISKCON, this wasn't just a case of trademark infringement – it was an affront to their faith.

ISKCON, renowned for its patience and peace-loving ethos, tried to resolve the matter amicably. They sent a series of notices to ISKCON Apparel, politely asking them to cease and desist. But their polite requests fell on deaf ears. It seemed the folks at ISKCON Apparel were determined to keep riding the wave of ISKCON's spiritual success. Faced with no other option, ISKCON decided to take the matter to court.

Legal Dispute

ISKCON's legal team argued that the acronym ISKCON wasn't just any trademark – it was a well-known one, globally recognized and revered. They pointed out that since its inception, ISKCON had invested heavily in promoting its name and logo through books, clothing, and other materials, all aimed at spreading Krishna consciousness. Their argument was simple, ISKCON's trademark was a spiritual asset, and unauthorized use not only diluted their brand but also misled the public. The plaintiffs emphasized that ISKCON's name and logo had become synonymous with their spiritual movement, and that the misuse of their trademark by the defendants could deceive followers and the public into believing that the products sold by ISKCON Apparel were officially sanctioned by ISKCON.

ISKCON Apparel Pvt. Ltd., which had by now rebranded itself as Alcis Sports Pvt. Ltd. (logo above), argued that they had already promised to stop using the ISKCON trademark. They maintained that they had changed their company name. However, the plaintiffs noted that the defendants continued to use the phrase "formerly known as ISKCON Apparel Pvt. Ltd." on their website.

Outcome

The court had to determine whether ISKCON's trademark was indeed well-known and if the defendants' actions constituted trademark infringement despite their name change.

The court recognized that ISKCON's trademark was not just a legal tool but a symbol of spiritual identity and community. Given ISKCON's extensive global presence and the goodwill associated with its name and logo, the court agreed that ISKCON's trademark deserved strong protection.

The judge noted that ISKCON had successfully demonstrated that their trademark was well-known and that the defendants' use of the name "ISKCON" was deliberate and intended to trade upon the reputation and goodwill developed by ISKCON.

The court ruled in favor of ISKCON, concluding that the defendants had indeed infringed upon ISKCON's trademark rights. The judge issued an injunction prohibiting the defendants from using the ISKCON trademark in any form, including the phrase "formerly known as ISKCON Apparel Pvt. Ltd."

The court emphasized that the term ISKCON was uniquely linked to the plaintiff and that its unauthorized use by the defendants could mislead the public and dilute the brand's spiritual significance. The verdict reaffirmed ISKCON's exclusive rights to its trademark and underscored the importance of protecting well-known trademarks from misuse.

So, the next time you see a Hare Krishna devotee dancing joyfully on the streets, remember that behind that serene smile is a community ready to defend its spiritual heritage with both devotion and determination.

Popcorn Buddha v. LesserEvil

v.

Background

Popcorn Buddha had been popping with its Buddha logo since 2011, blending peace, popcorn, and a pinch of Zen. But when LesserEvil, a national snack brand, started selling similar Buddha Bowl Foods branded popcorn, things got salty. Accusations of trademark infringement and misleading marketing popped up. Both companies used a Laughing Buddha figure in their logos, but Popcorn Buddha's logo had been in commercial use since 2011 (and registered in 2015), predating LesserEvil's use of "Buddha Bowl Foods" in 2015.

LesserEvil's marketing strategies also caused confusion, with their products appearing in online searches next to Popcorn Buddha's, despite Popcorn Buddha never selling their products on Amazon.

Legal Dispute

Popcorn Buddha argued that they were using their Popcorn Buddha mark first and should be able to stop others from using confusingly similar marks.

LesserEvil kept mum about the dispute but made subtle changes to their packaging after receiving a cease and desist order. Their new logo now featured just a serene Buddha bust, minus the word "Buddha," perhaps hoping to butter up their branding without stepping on spiritual toes.

Who truly owns the right to a Buddha with a bowl of popcorn? LesserEvil, while an established name in the snack scene since 2006, only trademarked "Buddha Bowl Foods" in 2015, with use beginning in 2014. This bowl of legalities centered around prior use, branding rights, and the complexities of trademarking cultural icons.

Outcome

Popcorn Buddha spent significant legal fees trying to protect its trademark, and due to slowing sales, they moved to Missouri from Pennsylvania. Lower taxes and proximity to their corn supplier in Missouri meant reduced costs and continued popcorn passion.

The case highlights the challenges small businesses face in protecting their trademarks against larger companies. Popcorn Buddha's relocation aims to mitigate financial losses and plan a future return, underscoring the impact of trademark disputes on small enterprises.

Chapter 14
Can't We All Just Coexist?

Sadly, the short answer is "No." It's like guests at a fancy dinner party, trademarks have their boundaries. Each one likes to be recognized and respected, ensuring no other brand encroaches on its unique identity. It's a bit like wearing a name tag that says, "Hello, my name is Trademark, and I'm unique!" The problem is, if everyone tried to share or blend these tags, the whole shindig would turn into a confusing mess of mismatched identities and awkward introductions.

Now, take the trademark for "COEXIST." You'd think that a trademark with such a peace-loving, inclusive name would be all about letting others share the spotlight. But even "coexist" can't just let any partygoer waltz in and use its name without a formal introduction and permission. It's like the trademark for "coexist" is saying, "Hey, I love harmony and togetherness, but I still need my space and recognition!" This may sound paradoxical, but it's essential for maintaining the order and clarity of the trademark party, ensuring that every guest knows who's who and what's what.

In the end, trademarks are like party planners with a strict guest list policy. They make sure everyone has a good time without stepping on each other's toes—or logos. So, while it might seem ironic that "coexist" can't let others simply coexist without permission, it's all part of the grand dance to keep the trademark soirée from turning into a chaotic jamboree. After all, every trademark deserves its moment to shine under the disco ball, and a well-organized party ensures that each one gets its fair share of the limelight. So we'll end this book with the case of Coexist v. Cafepress to see how much trademark coexistence can happen!

Coexist v. Cafepress

Background

In a quirky clash of commerce and creativity, Coexist, LLP, known for its famous "COEXIST" design featuring religious and peace symbols, found itself in a legal tussle with Cafepress.com, an online marketplace where users create and sell custom merchandise. Cafepress had allowed its users to create and sell products bearing the "COEXIST" design without Coexist, LLP's permission, prompting the company to file a lawsuit.

Legal Dispute

Coexist, LLP claimed that Cafepress.com was infringing on its trademark by allowing third-party vendors to use the "COEXIST" design without authorization. They argued that this unauthorized use diluted their brand and caused consumer confusion.

Cafepress contended that it was merely a platform for user-generated content and was not directly responsible for the designs uploaded by its users. They argued that they were protected under the Digital Millennium Copyright Act (DMCA) as an intermediary service provider.

The case hinged on the interpretation of trademark infringement and the responsibilities of online platforms under the DMCA.

The court had to determine whether Cafepress's actions constituted direct infringement or if they were protected as an intermediary platform. The key issue was whether Cafepress had control over the content and if it took adequate measures to prevent infringement.

Cafepress argued that they complied with the DMCA by providing a mechanism for copyright holders to request the removal of infringing content. The court examined whether Cafepress had acted promptly upon receiving infringement notices from Coexist, LLP.

Outcome

In a decision that balanced legal principles with a touch of humor, the court ruled that Cafepress had to implement stricter controls to prevent the sale of infringing "COEXIST" merchandise, but did not hold them liable for past infringements.

Cafepress agreed to enhance its content monitoring systems and to work more closely with trademark holders to protect their rights. Coexist, LLP and Cafepress reached an agreement to collaborate on future designs, allowing Cafepress to sell authorized "COEXIST" merchandise while ensuring that Coexist, LLP received proper recognition and compensation. The case ended on a positive note, with both parties committed to spreading the message of peace and coexistence through their creative endeavors.

www.ingramcontent.com/pod-product-compliance
Lightning Source LLC
Chambersburg PA
CBHW070147230526
45471CB00002B/548